Unleashing Your Infinite Potential

A Journey Through Think and Grow Rich

Brian McGinty

Inspired by Napoleon Hill and Bob Proctor

UNLEASHING YOUR INFINITE POTENTIAL

First edition. June 9, 2023.

Copyright © 2023 BMcGinty.

ISBN: 979-8223328230

Written by BMcGinty.

Table of Contents

Dedication

This book is a humble tribute to the enduring memory of Napoleon Hill, the visionary author of *Think and Grow Rich*, whose wisdom continues to resonate in every word I pen. Further, I extend this dedication to Bob Proctor, a beacon of light in my life who generously guided me as my mentor for a decade until his poignant departure from this world in 2022. His influence in my life will forever be cherished.

Above all, my deepest dedication is reserved for my loving wife, Emma, and our extraordinary children—Caogain, Emily, Bryony, and Jimmy. They are the heartbeat that fuels my ambitions, and the priceless joy that keeps me grounded. They inspire me every day to strive towards leaving this world a better, brighter place than I was privileged to inherit. This book, like every endeavour of mine, is a testament to the love and inspiration they bring into my life.

Foreword

This book was inspired by my amazing results over a ten-year period, achieved by using the thirteen principles found within *Think and Grow Rich* and by having Bob Proctor as my mentor.

In 2013 I found myself homeless, living in a foreign country. I had lost my business. My wife, Emma, was pregnant, diagnosed with chronic fatigue at twenty-seven, and couldn't work. She had been working as a Christian missionary in Tanzania for seven years, became very ill with malaria, and had to return home.

Her mother had also passed away from ovarian cancer, my mother had been diagnosed with Alzheimer's, and my best friend had died suddenly. To say things were bad was an understatement.

By divine intervention, a friend asked me to read a copy of *Think and Grow Rich*, which I declined as, "I don't read books". We all take in information in different ways, and reading was not my favourite.

Thankfully he insisted and explained how I could listen to it free on Audible, so for some reason, I did. To say that decision changed my life is an understatement.

I quickly learned that all my problems could be solved from within, and my results were simply a reflection of my thoughts and actions up to that point. That's not something many are willing to acknowledge and accept, but for some reason I took that on board.

For anything to get better, I had to get better, and my dire circumstances meant that had to happen fast.

One immediate piece of advice I acted on was to write down what I was grateful for and do it every day. This simple action started me on an amazing road to abundance and happiness that I have been on ever since.

We now have four fantastic children, Emma's health is improving every year, and we live in a beautiful home in the sun overlooking the Mediterranean. I have grown and developed multiple million-dollar businesses and have total time freedom through multiple passive income streams.

Although I don't need to work for financial reasons, I know from experience that true happiness comes from contribution and serving others. With that in mind, I decided to dedicate my future to paying it forward and sharing what I have learned with others. Bob taught the principles found in *Think and Grow Rich* since the 1960s, and it was his sudden death in February 2022 that gave me the urge to pick up his torch and not let it go out.

I could have, and was about to, become one of his consultants when he said something in one of his *Six Minutes to Success* videos that changed my path. He said, "If a goal doesn't make you grow, it is not a goal, and working as a sales consultant was not something new to me". I had been successful in this area with multiple companies over the years.

The thought, however, of running my own company, writing this book, creating courses, and mentoring people globally certainly made me uncomfortable, so that was the direction I decided to take.

Over the years I have completed courses by The Proctor Gallagher Institute, Global Sciences Foundation, NeuroGym, Mindvalley, Tony Robbins, and others, so my practical knowledge in this area is wide and varied. I say practical knowledge because knowledge is not power; it's just gathering information. The world's universities have many unhappy, broke professors. Applying knowledge is where the power lies.

More recently I have created my **Get a Life** Mentoring brand, https://getalife.info, and become a Certified Living the Legacy Mentor in partnership with The *Think and Grow Rich* Movie company. Our aim is to spread awareness of the principles of the book through movies, global events, and various courses for private and corporate audiences.

One of the first observations I made when introducing people to *Think and Grow Rich* was that there was a need for a shorter version, especially for "non-readers". Not to mention the ever-shortening concentration span of the modern-day audience. Three hundred pages or nine and a half hours on Audible was a bridge too far for some, so I set about creating a solution. This was to take the key points from each chapter and distil the wisdom into easy segments with inspiration from Napoleon and Bob, sprinkled with my own thoughts and observations.

My vision for this publication is, therefore, to provide a coffee table overview of *Think and Grow Rich* that you can pick up and read every day, one that is also short enough for the Audible listeners out there who want to grab a quick chapter while driving to work or doing the household chores.

I will always recommend reading and re-reading *Think and Grow Rich* at your earliest convenience, as it is something you will want to go through more than once. Bob read the book for over sixty years, and I have been listening to it every week for ten years because we both realised that learning never ends and memory must be refreshed.

A way I like to teach this process is the following: If you are standing at the window, the view from the first floor of a building is different than on the twentieth. Every time you read the book, you climb the floors, getting a better view of the world each time and a different perspective on each chapter.

Life has an unlimited number of floors, so every time you read this book and/or the longer version, you will see something you have not seen before. It is an amazing process and not one I fully appreciated until I started doing it myself.

If you want to get the best from this experience, or the full book, highlight any words or phrases that resonate with you so you can easily find them again. Even better, at the end of each chapter, take ten minutes to write down what you have understood about the information and how you could use it in your own life.

"If you think it, ink it", and, **"The word was made flesh"**, are not famous lincs for nothing! There is power in saying words out loud and putting them on paper. Try it as you complete each chapter, and I think you will be surprised at the results.

I hope you enjoy and get great value from my first literary exploration and it can set you and your family on a wonderful path to health, wealth, and happiness. With all that in mind, let's get started and begin to discover more about Napoleon, Bob, and the magic I discovered within *Think and Grow Rich*.

Brian McGinty

Introduction

What would you like to improve in your life? Would you like more money, more time, better relationships, better health? I have learned over the years from personal experience that there is no point in having one without the others.

As my wife's caregiver over the last thirteen years, I know that a healthy person has many wishes, while a sick person has one. I also know that there is no point in being miserable in your mansion or driving your Ferrari on your own.

The good news is that Think and Grow Rich will show you how to become rich in wealth, health, and, most importantly, personal happiness. True richness is having all three.

You don't need to take my word for how effective it is either. It has been changing lives for decades on a global scale, affecting literally millions of people since it was first published in 1937.

One of the reasons I really took notice of the information was the impressive list of names from the early 1900s who recommended its content. *Think and Grow Rich* is not theory; it is a research document, full of true stories, quotes, and real information gathered from some of the greatest brains of the early twentieth century.

In more recent times, many people have credited Napoleon Hill's "Think and Grow Rich" as a significant influence on their journey to wealth and happiness.

A few of those are as follows:

· **Daymond John, founder of FUBU and TV personality on *Shark Tank*:** "I've probably read the book twenty times. It was very instrumental in my success".

· **Jim Rohn, motivational speaker:** "I found the book to be very interesting, as it helped me understand how powerful the mind can be".

· **Tony Robbins, life and business strategist:** "Napoleon Hill's philosophy teaches you what you were meant to be and helps unfold your true potential".

· **Grant Cardone, sales expert:** "*Think and Grow Rich* was the first book I read that connected the dots between thinking and living a great life".

· **Brian Tracy, self-development author:** "This book gave me ideas and strategies that transformed my life and career".

· **Dennis Kimbro, author and success expert:** "When it comes to success literature, Napoleon Hill's work is the benchmark".

· **Jack Canfield, co-creator of the Chicken Soup for the Soul Series:** "Hill's *Think and Grow Rich* has had a significant influence on my life, contributing to my success".

· **Les Brown, motivational speaker:** "*Think and Grow Rich* changed my mindset and set me on the path to success".

· **Bob Proctor, personal development guru:** "This book had a significant influence on my life. The understanding of its principles is what separates the successful from those who fail to reach their goals".

· **John C. Maxwell, leadership expert:** "Reading *Think and Grow Rich* by Napoleon Hill was a game-changer for me. It made me realize that success begins and ends in the mind".

These quotes are paraphrased and reflect the essence of the impact *Think and Grow Rich* had on these individuals rather than their exact words. The central theme, however, remains consistent – that Napoleon Hill's work played an instrumental role in shaping their success.

Chapter 1
The Man Behind the Masterpiece: Napoleon Hill

In the chronicles of personal development and self-improvement, few names resonate as profoundly as Napoleon Hill. Known for his ground-breaking work, Hill's influence continues to shape the lives of individuals worldwide, inspiring them to overcome obstacles and manifest their deepest desires.

Napoleon was born into poverty in a one-room cabin in Pound, Virginia, on October 26, 1883. The trials of his early life could have easily written a narrative of defeat and struggle. However, Hill was not one to be swayed by circumstances. Instead, he chose to chart his own destiny, transforming adversities into stepping stones for success.

It may be a stepping-stone or a stumbling block, depending on the mental attitude with which it is faced.

—Napoleon Hill

His journey into the world of success literature began in 1908 when he was assigned to interview the steel magnate Andrew Carnegie for a magazine. Carnegie, impressed by Hill's keen interest and probing questions, saw in him the perfect candidate for a special task. He proposed that Hill spend twenty years interviewing the wealthiest and most successful people to discover a simple formula for success. Hill, despite the daunting nature of the task and the fact it offered no monetary compensation, accepted. This choice marked the turning point of his life.

Over the ensuing two decades, Hill interviewed over five hundred successful people, including Henry Ford, Thomas Edison, Alexander Graham Bell, John D. Rockefeller, and Theodore Roosevelt. From these interactions, he gleaned the principles of success that would become the foundation of his work.

Hill's first significant work, *The Law of Success*, was published in 1928. It comprised eight volumes and laid out sixteen key principles for success. Despite its initial impact, it was his subsequent work, *Think and Grow Rich*, published amidst the backdrop of the Great Depression in 1937, that cemented his legacy. The book offered an accessible and practical guide to achieving success and has since sold millions of copies globally.

However, Hill's life wasn't devoid of challenges. He faced numerous personal and professional setbacks, including business failures and the loss of his personal fortune more than once. Yet, embodying the principles he preached, Hill saw each defeat as a temporary setback and an opportunity for learning.

Napoleon Hill passed away in November 1970, but his legacy continues to inspire and guide people towards personal and professional success. His work forms the bedrock of personal development literature, influencing countless authors and motivational speakers, including the esteemed Bob Proctor, who often referred to Hill's work in his teachings.

Hill's life and work illustrate a key message: our backgrounds and circumstances do not define us; rather our beliefs, desires, and persistence shape our destiny. It's a message of hope and empowerment, reminding us that no matter our starting point, we can all think and grow rich. His principles are not just about financial wealth, but about cultivating a rich and fulfilling life.

As we delve deeper into Hill's masterpiece, let's carry with us the spirit of his journey – a journey marked by resilience, a relentless quest for knowledge, and an unwavering belief in the potential of the human mind. It's this spirit that continues to light our path to riches, urging us to dream, to strive, and to manifest our grandest desires.

Napoleon Hill once said, "Whatever the mind can conceive and believe, it can achieve." With this guiding philosophy, let's embark on our exploration of his life-altering wisdom.

Chapter 2
The Torchbearer of Transformation: Bob Proctor

As we traverse the landscape of personal development, the path is often illuminated by influential figures who have not only walked the journey but continue to light the way for others. One such figure, who embodied the principles of self-improvement and abundant living, was Bob Proctor.

Bob was born on July 5, 1934, in Ontario, Canada, and his story is a testament to the transformative power of thought. As a young man, he struggled with discontent and financial instability, bouncing from job to job, seeking a sense of purpose and prosperity that eluded him.

In 1961, a friend introduced him to Napoleon Hill's *Think and Grow Rich*. The book resonated with Bob profoundly. Its message sparked a profound transformation within him, driving him to study the book intensely and implement its teachings in his life. The result was a spectacular turnaround. In just a year, Bob's income increased manifold, and he moved up in his career, joining the Nightingale-Conant organization.

Bob's personal transformation ignited within him a passion to help others unlock their potential and achieve their goals. His subsequent journey as a motivational speaker, author, consultant, coach, and mentor has been fuelled by this enduring passion.

The core of Bob's teaching revolves around the power of thought and the mind's potential to create reality. Drawing from his comprehensive study of *Think and Grow Rich* and other works in the personal development realm, Bob Proctor emphasized the principles of success and abundance, including the law of attraction, the power of positive thinking, and the importance of setting and pursuing clear, definite goals.

Over the decades, Bob played a pivotal role in the personal development industry. His book, *You Were Born Rich*, furthers the principles of personal achievement and has influenced countless people around the globe.

Despite his success, Bob remained a lifelong student of human potential and personal development. His humility and relentless quest for knowledge remind us that the journey of self-improvement and success is an ongoing process, not a destination. His life embodied the transformative power of the principles that Napoleon Hill laid out in *Think and Grow Rich*. Through his teachings, he brought these principles to life for me and for modern audiences, showing us that we all possess the power to shape our destinies.

As we delve deeper into the wisdom of *Think and Grow Rich*, Bob's inspirational journey serves as a beacon, reminding us that we are not passive spectators but active creators of our lives. As Bob often said, "If you can see it in your mind, you can hold it in your hand."

As we proceed, let's carry this empowering thought with us, allowing it to guide our understanding, shape our mindset, and fuel our pursuit of a rich and fulfilling life. After all, as we learn from the lives of Napoleon Hill and Bob Proctor, as well as my own, the journey to abundance starts within, in the fertile grounds of our mind.

Chapter 3
What Is the Essence of Think and Grow Rich?

Think and Grow Rich has transformed the lives of countless individuals for decades, and its teachings continue to inspire people around the world to this day.

In this book, Hill shares the success secrets of some of the most influential and wealthy people of his time, distilling their wisdom into a powerful blueprint for achievement that is just as relevant today as it was when the book was first published.

The book is divided into fifteen chapters, each focusing on a different aspect of the success mindset. He begins by stressing the importance of having a burning desire to achieve one's goals, followed by the role of faith and the power of auto-suggestion in manifesting that desire into reality.

Next, Hill emphasizes the need for specialized knowledge, imagination, and organized planning, which, when combined with decision, persistence, and the power of the mastermind, can lead to extraordinary success.

Hill also reveals the secret of sex transmutation and the power of the subconscious mind in achieving one's goals. He then delves into the workings of the brain and how one can use their sixth sense to gain insights and make decisions that lead to success.

Finally, Hill provides practical strategies to overcome the six ghosts of fear that hold many people back from achieving their dreams. By following the principles laid out in this book, anyone can unlock their full potential and achieve extraordinary success in their personal and professional life.

Think and Grow Rich is a book that can transform the way you think and help you achieve the success you desire. It is a timeless classic that should be read and re-read by anyone who wants to live their best life and leave a wonderful legacy.

As Bob often said, "If you can dream it, you can achieve it. Your thoughts and beliefs create your reality, and with the right mindset, anything is possible."

Chapter 4
Summary of Napoleon Hill's Preface

In the preface of *Think and Grow Rich*, Napoleon Hill sets the stage for the profound journey the reader is about to embark upon. He explains that the book was inspired by his meeting with the great industrialist Andrew Carnegie, who believed that success could be achieved by anyone who understood and applied a certain set of principles.

Hill, who spent over twenty years researching and interviewing some of the most successful people in history, reveals that these principles are not limited to just one profession or industry. Instead, they can be applied by anyone, regardless of their background, education, or circumstances.

Some of these famous individuals include the following:

· **Andrew Carnegie** – a Scottish-American businessman and philanthropist who built a vast steel empire in the late nineteenth century.

· **Thomas Edison** – an American inventor credited with developing many important devices, including the phonograph and the incandescent light bulb.

· **Henry Ford** – an American businessman and founder of the Ford Motor Company, known for revolutionizing the automobile industry with the development of the assembly line.

· **John D. Rockefeller** – an American businessman and philanthropist who founded the Standard Oil Company, which became one of the largest and most powerful companies in the world.

· **Charles M. Schwab** – an American steel magnate who rose to prominence in the late nineteenth and early twentieth centuries, and later became president of Bethlehem Steel.

· **Theodore Roosevelt** – the twenty-sixth president of the United States, known for his progressive policies and efforts to conserve natural resources.

· **William Wrigley Jr.** – an American businessman who founded the Wrigley Company, which became known for its chewing gum.

· **Elbert H. Gary** – an American lawyer and businessman who played a key role in the development of the steel industry and later became the first chairman of the United States Steel Corporation.

These individuals were all highly successful and influential in their respective fields, and Hill studied them to understand the principles and habits that led to their success. The full list is amazing when you think of who they were and the times they lived in. Electricity, communication, TV, radio, cars, flight, sciences, medicines, and much more were all developed by these people from mere ideas!

How did ordinary people with often little education do such extraordinary things? Napoleon Hill made it his life's work to find out, and we have been blessed with the fruit of his work.

Chapter 5
Hill's Introduction

In the introduction to *Think and Grow Rich*, Napoleon Hill begins by setting the tone for the entire book, as he outlines the core philosophy that drives success. In this chapter, the author establishes the concept of "thoughts becoming things" and the power of the mind to create success in any area of life.

Bob often referred to this chapter as the foundation of his teaching, as it emphasizes the importance of having a clear, definite goal and the willingness to do whatever it takes to achieve it.

Hill uses examples of successful individuals, such as Andrew Carnegie, to illustrate the principles of success. Hill's research identified a set of principles that successful people use, which are known as the *thirteen steps to riches*. These principles are presented throughout the book, and they are the key to unlocking success.

There are many references in the book to many great people and events. It was particularly interesting for me, as an avid collector of old Fords, that Napoleon includes a great story about Henry Ford in the introduction.

This recalled the time when Ford's engineers told him that producing a V8 engine was impossible, yet he told them, "Make it anyway", and eventually they did. This is one example that encapsulates many of the principles we learn about in later chapters.

Chapter 6
The Thirteen Principles

For over twenty years, Napoleon Hill interviewed and studied the great and the good of his time.

Just imagine how much it would cost for you or me to spend the next twenty years interviewing Elon Musk, Richard Branson, Jeff Bezos, Warren Buffet, Oprah Winfrey, and other successful business leaders.

The good news is that the principles are the same today as they were then and will apply the same in another hundred years' time.

We are just fortunate to have this distilled knowledge at our fingertips. It comes in thirteen easy-to-remember principles that, when used together, can lead anyone to a life of abundance and happiness.

The thirteen principles are as follows:

1. Desire

2. Faith

3. Auto-suggestion

4. Specialised knowledge

5. Imagination

6. Organised planning

7. Decision

8. Persistence

9. Power of the mastermind

10. The mystery of sex transmutation

11. The subconscious mind

12. The brain

13. The sixth sense

Let's take a deeper dive into each chapter and discover the key points so you can learn them as quickly as possible. I will also add my favourite quote on each principle and some of my own thoughts and those that I learned from Bob.

1: Desire

The starting point of all achievement is desire.

—Napoleon Hill

To get started, Hill explains the power of desire and its role in achieving success. He argues that desire is the starting point of all achievement and that without a burning desire for something, you lack the motivation and persistence necessary to reach your goals.

Hill defines desire as a strong, intense, and burning longing for something that you are willing to work hard to attain. He emphasizes that desire must be specific and well-defined and that you must have a clear picture of what you want if you are going to achieve it.

One of the key points that Hill makes in this chapter is that desire must be accompanied by a plan of action. He argues that desire alone is not enough to achieve success and that you must also develop a specific plan for achieving your goals and take consistent action towards them.

Hill also emphasizes the importance of persistence in the pursuit of your desires. He argues that setbacks and obstacles are inevitable but that the most successful people are those who can stay focused on their goals and persist through difficulties.

In his own teachings, Bob Proctor often emphasizes the power of desire and its ability to transform your life. He argues that desire is the starting point of all achievement and that it is essential to have a clear and specific vision of what you want.

Bob also stresses the importance of faith and belief in your ability to achieve your goals. He argues that limiting beliefs and self-doubt can hold you back from achieving your desires and that it is essential to develop a positive mindset and belief system. Also emphasised is the importance of taking action towards your goals and persisting through difficulties. He argues that success is a process and requires consistent effort and dedication over time.

We are provided with a powerful and inspiring message about the importance of desire and its role in achieving success, as well as practical strategies on how to achieve it.

Over the years I have learned that many people have lots of wants and needs but not many desires. I believe that if you really desire something, it changes you emotionally. Think about someone or something you wanted in the past that was the last thing you thought about at night and the first thing you thought about in the morning, something that you craved so much that you had to achieve it no matter long it took. That is a desire.

Desires *should* scare you; they should help you stretch and grow.

In 2013 I was homeless and had no money but a strong desire to provide security for my wife and children. This desire helped me overcome worry, tiredness, disappointment, and failures along the way and was the wind in my sails that carried me to success.

Tune into your desires and harness their power.

2: Faith

Faith is the eternal elixir, it gives life, power and action to the impulse of thought.

—Napoleon Hill

In this chapter, Napoleon Hill explores the concept of faith and its importance in achieving success. Hill defines faith as a "state of mind which may be induced, or created, by affirmations or repeated instructions to the subconscious mind." He argues that faith is essential for success and that without it, you will lack the confidence and resilience necessary to overcome obstacles and achieve your goals.

Hill also emphasizes the importance of having a definite purpose in order to cultivate faith. He argues that having a clear and specific goal in mind is essential for developing faith and that without a goal, your efforts will lack direction and focus.

One of the key points that Hill makes in this chapter is that faith must be accompanied by action. He argues that faith alone is not enough to achieve success and that you must also take consistent action towards your goals in order to bring them to fruition.

Hill also discusses the importance of persistence and resilience in cultivating faith. He argues that setbacks and failures are inevitable but that the most successful people are those who can stay focused on their goals and persist through difficulties.

In his teachings, Bob often emphasizes the importance of faith and its ability to transform your life. He argues that faith is a state of mind that can be cultivated through positive affirmations and a belief in yourself and your abilities.

Proctor also stresses the importance of having a definite purpose and taking action towards your goals. He argues that without a clear and specific goal in mind, your efforts will lack direction and focus and that taking consistent action towards your goals is essential for achieving success.

Never forget the importance of persistence and resilience in cultivating faith. Setbacks and failures are inevitable, but the most successful people are those who can stay focused on their goals and persist through difficulties. For all people, in all stages of life, this chapter provides practical strategies for cultivating faith and using it to achieve success.

Growing up in 97 percent Catholic Ireland, during "the troubles", in a family of funeral directors, faith was a big part of my life. Having death on the news, and in my life, every day made people think about their own mortality more than many of us do today.

It wasn't until I read *Think and Grow Rich* and was introduced to Bob Proctor that my concept of faith was expanded and I really understood that faith isn't just about faith in an afterlife but has to do with how we live our everyday lives.

For most of my life I was merely hoping and wishing that things would happen through prayer without really understanding the power of faith.

I have also concluded that not all Churches teach people about the true power of faith but simply give the congregation enough information to ensure they come back and put some money in the bowl again next Sunday. This is not true in all cases, but it can be seen as a theme in many religions of the world.

Even those with no apparent faith in any organised religion would agree with the scientists that everything is created from energy. Energy is omnipresent in all places, cannot be created or destroyed and constantly moves through form. Some would give "God" the same description.

Getting back to faith in terms that I understand as a Christian, I believe that we are made in God's image, but we have made the mistake of trying to make God in our image. My faith in God and therefore myself is stronger than ever, and I believe we have the individual power to be and do whatever we want.

Even if you are not religious, I think everyone needs to understand the power of these words in relation to faith:

Ask, and it shall be given you; seek, and ye. shall find; knock, and it shall be opened unto you: For everyone that asketh receiveth; and he that seeketh, findeth; and to him that knocketh it shall be opened (Matt. 7-7:8 KJV).

Try asking, seeking, and knocking through life with desire and faith, and the results might just surprise you. Remember, however, that, "Faith without works is dead", simply means that if you have faith but are taking no action, you are just wishing.

I have been practicing this for ten years, and I am not surprised by anything anymore. The health, wealth, and happiness have all been delivered just as I had faith they would when I took action to achieve them.

3: Auto-Suggestion

Auto-suggestion is the agency of control through which an individual may voluntarily feed his subconscious mind on thoughts of a creative nature, or, by neglect, permit thoughts of a destructive nature to find their way into this rich garden of the mind.

—Napoleon Hill

Napoleon next explores the concept of *auto-suggestion* and defines it as the process by which you can influence your subconscious mind through repeated affirmations or suggestions.

Hill argues that auto-suggestion is a powerful tool, as it allows you to reprogram your subconscious mind and overcome limiting beliefs and negative thought patterns. He emphasizes that the subconscious mind is the "connecting link" between the individual and the universal mind and that by using auto-suggestion, you can tap into the power of the universe and manifest your desires.

One of the key points that Hill makes in this chapter is that auto-suggestion must be accompanied by belief to be effective. He argues that if you repeat affirmations or suggestions without truly believing in them, they will have little impact on your subconscious mind.

Hill also discusses the importance of emotion in auto-suggestion. He argues that for suggestions to be effective, they must be accompanied by strong positive emotions such as faith, love, and enthusiasm.

In his teachings, Bob often emphasized the power of auto-suggestion and its ability to transform your life. He argued that auto-suggestion is a powerful tool for reprogramming your subconscious mind and overcoming limiting beliefs and negative thought patterns. He also stressed the importance of belief and emotion in auto-suggestion. He argued that for suggestions to be effective, you must believe in them wholeheartedly and feel the positive emotions associated with them.

Overall, we learn from Napoleon and Bob that repetition is the key factor in mastering auto-suggestion. Repeating affirmations or suggestions daily is essential for reprogramming your subconscious mind and creating new positive habits and thought patterns.

I have found that the average person finds the concept of auto-suggestion difficult because we now live in a world of instant results. Clicking an app and swiping left to find a date are great, but they will never help you change the hard-wired programming in your subconscious mind.

The whole concept of auto-suggestion relies on us being able to repeat a task consistently over a period and create a brand-new habit. I have been practicing this for ten years with my bedside Gratitude book, but I admit that it is not filled in every day due to various factors, including my wife being ill, dealing with children, or simply forgetting.

However, we must not look at temporary defeat as failure. Everyone has bad days and sometimes bad weeks. What is important is that if we get blown off course, we get back on course as quickly as possible.

Some effective techniques I teach to aid in auto-suggestion are firstly to buy a gratitude book and try to fill it in every night before going off to sleep. In the morning, put it on your pillow so that you physically must remove it to sleep.

When you are filling in your gratitude book each night, start with the following sentence I learned from Bob:

"I am so happy and grateful now that I am/can . . ."

I always start with "happy, healthy, fit, and free and continue with listing my desires in the present tense. If you write them in the future tense, that's where they will remain.

I have also found that the shower or gym are great places to create a ritual, such as saying the following:

"Every day, and in every way, I am getting better and better and better".

As a final tip, putting Post-it *notes* on the bathroom mirror with some positive affirmations is a great way to remind yourself to auto-suggest whatever you want to hard-wire into your mind.

Ultimately you want to create a habit as strong as tying your shoes or driving. These are things you don't think about anymore; you just do them, as they are part of who you are.

Start with one thing you would like to be or become and use auto-suggestion mixed with faith and desire to achieve it. This is what creates the new habit, the new paradigm, and the new you.

4: Specialized Knowledge

An educated man is not, necessarily, one who has an abundance of general or specialized knowledge. An educated man is one who has so developed the faculties of his mind that he may acquire anything he wants, or its equivalent, without violating the rights of others.

—Napoleon Hill

In this chapter, Napoleon Hill emphasizes the importance of specialized knowledge. He argues that general knowledge is not enough to succeed in a specific field and that you must have specialized knowledge to stand out and achieve great results.

Hill defines specialized knowledge as "knowledge which one has acquired through a personal experience or a specialized training in a particular field." He emphasizes that specialized knowledge is essential for achieving success, as it allows you to offer unique solutions and stand out from the competition.

One of the key points Hill makes in this chapter is that specialized knowledge can be acquired through study and practice. He argues that anyone can acquire specialized knowledge by investing time and effort into studying and practicing in a specific field.

Hill also discusses the importance of collaboration in acquiring specialized knowledge. He argues that you can learn from others who have already acquired specialized knowledge and that collaborating with experts in your field can accelerate your learning and help you achieve success faster.

In his teachings, Bob Proctor emphasized the importance of specialized knowledge and its ability to set you apart from the competition. He explained that general knowledge is not enough to achieve great results in a specific field and that you must invest time and effort into acquiring specialized knowledge to stand out and succeed.

Bob also stressed the importance of continuous learning in acquiring specialized knowledge. He argued that the world is constantly changing and that it is essential to stay up-to-date with the latest trends and developments in your field to remain competitive.

Like Hill, Proctor emphasizes the importance of collaboration in acquiring specialized knowledge. He shows us that you can learn from others who have already acquired specialized knowledge and that networking with experts in your field can accelerate your learning and help you achieve success faster.

Throughout this chapter you will learn practical strategies for acquiring specialized knowledge and standing out from the competition.

In my experience it takes time to acquire specialist knowledge, but that should not be a reason to put it off. It is also very important to find a subject that you have a passion for because it will make the process so much easier and enjoyable.

Over the years I have acquired specialist knowledge in insurance, property, precious metals, and blockchain technology, as well as my ever-continuing exploration of *Think and Grow Rich* and similar works.

It took me several years of learning, listening to, or reading Bob's many recommendations and doing many courses to gather the knowledge I now have in this area. With advances in science, we are learning more about how the mind works, and so my learning continues and will for the rest of my life.

Think about something you are really interested in and start to become an expert in that field yourself. If you do not have the specialist knowledge in any area, you can always find, collaborate, and even pay for the people who have the knowledge you need to achieve your goals.

As I write this book, we are entering the AI age, where you can have all the knowledge you need at your fingertips. With such a fantastic resource at our disposal, this makes this principle of obtaining specialised knowledge one of the easiest for us to master.

5: Imagination

The imagination is the most powerful, miraculous, inconceivably powerful force that the world's ever known.

—Napoleon Hill

Next up, Hill discusses the power of imagination in achieving success. He argues that imagination is the starting point for all great achievements, as it allows us to visualize and create the future we desire.

Hill defines imagination as the "workshop of the mind," where all plans and ideas are created. He emphasizes that imagination is not just a tool for artists and creatives but is essential for anyone looking to achieve success in any area of life.

One of the key points that Hill makes in this chapter is that imagination is not limited by our current circumstances or past experiences. He argues that we have the power to imagine and create a future that is different from our current reality and that this is the first step towards achieving our goals.

Bob shows us the importance of imagination by explaining that our thoughts and beliefs shape our reality and that imagination is the tool we use to create our desired reality.

He taught us that we can use our imagination to visualize our goals and create a mental image of the life we desire. He emphasized the importance of clarity in our imagination and encouraged us to use all our senses to create a vivid mental picture of our desired reality.

Like Hill, Proctor explained that imagination is not limited by our current circumstances or past experiences. He showed that we have the power to imagine and create a new reality for ourselves, no matter where we currently are in life.

This chapter offers valuable insights into the power of imagination and provides practical strategies for harnessing this power and creating the future you desire. When I think about imagination, I always think of the quote from Marty Rubin: "Blessed are the dreamers for they keep the rest of us awake".

Where would we be without Edison's thoughts of the lightbulb, Marconi's dream of sending voices through the air, or the Wright Brothers imagining themselves flying through the sky?

There is a lot of talk in the world about AI now, so this chapter should help people clearly see the limitations of this technology. We, as humans, are creative beings in that we can originate new ideas, dreams, and visions of the future. Machines are not connected to infinite intelligence, God, or whatever name you choose and can only work with information that already exists.

Put simply, we have the power of imagination with our other higher faculties, which are will, intuition, memory, reason, and perception, which I will touch on again later. Look around the room you are in: everything you see started off in someone's imagination, and this, for me, is one of the most important ideas I grasped from *Think and Grow Rich*. As children, we are told to use our imagination, but as soon as we get to adulthood, we are told to stop dreaming and fit in.

All through my life, I was always told by teachers and others that I was a dreamer, full of big ideas, but that I needed to get back to reality. Thank God I didn't listen, and I continue to imagine and dream to this day. It took me until my mid-thirties and an understanding of the thirteen principles to realise that I could use imagination in conjunction with the other principles to have whatever life I wanted to create.

Try it: Imagine where you desire to be in twelve months 'time, keep reminding yourself that you already there, have faith, take action towards it, and watch it happen.

6: Organized Planning

The successful leader must plan his work and work his plan. A leader who moves by guesswork, without practical definite plans, is comparable to a ship without a rudder. Sooner or later, he will land on the rocks.

—Napoleon Hill

In this chapter, Napoleon Hill discusses the importance of organized planning in achieving your goals. He argues that without a well-defined plan, our efforts will be scattered and we will not achieve the results we desire.

Hill defines organized planning as "the crystallization of desire into action". He emphasizes the importance of having a clear goal and a detailed plan for achieving that goal. He also stresses the importance of flexibility in our plans, as we may need to adjust them based on changing circumstances.

Bob taught us that our thoughts and beliefs shape our realities and that planning is the tool we use to turn our thoughts and beliefs into action.

He explained that a well-defined plan is essential for achieving any goal, whether it is financial success, personal development, or any other area of life. He encouraged us to set clear and specific goals and to break them down into smaller, more manageable tasks.

He also emphasized the importance of taking consistent action towards our goals. He showed that taking small, consistent steps is the key to making progress and achieving success.

Like Hill, Proctor stressed the importance of flexibility in our plans. He made it clear that we may encounter obstacles and challenges along the way and that we need to be adaptable in our approach if we are to overcome them.

We can see events as stumbling blocks or stepping stones; it all depends on how we use them!

As a self-confessed dreamer, I have never been enthused by the word *organised*, so this chapter forced me to learn some new skills. By using the techniques and tips provided by Napoleon and Bob, I was able to turn these new organisational skills into habitual behaviour.

One major tip everyone can take on board is that there is power in putting pen to paper. I have found that the act of writing the words down gives life to them almost in a magical way that cannot be achieved digitally.

A captain always knows exactly where the ship is going before it leaves port; the aeroplane always has a flight plan. If they didn't, they would soon end up on the rocks somewhere, so don't let your life do the same. You are the captain of your life. Plot the course and use organised planning to get there.

7: Decision

Men who succeed reach decisions promptly, and change them, if at all, very slowly. Men who fail, reach decisions, if at all, very slowly, and change them frequently, and quickly.

—Napoleon Hill

For decision, Hill explains the importance of making timely and definite decisions in achieving success. He argues that indecision is one of the major causes of failure and that successful people are decisive in their actions.

Hill defines decision as "the mastery of procrastination" and argues that successful people make decisions quickly and stick to them. He also stresses the importance of being persistent in our decisions, even in the face of obstacles and challenges.

Bob also showed us the importance of taking timely and definite decisions in achieving whatever goals we set for ourselves. He believed, as do I, that our ability to make decisions is one of the most important factors in determining our success.

Research shows us that successful people are decisive and act quickly. Indecision and procrastination are major obstacles to achieving our goals, and we must develop the habit of making decisions quickly and confidently.

Bob also stressed the importance of taking responsibility for our decisions. He taught us that we cannot blame others for the outcomes of our decisions and that we must own our decisions and take action accordingly.

This chapter provides us with valuable insights into the importance of decision-making in achieving success. Here you will learn practical strategies for developing the habit of making timely and definite decisions. By mastering the art of decision-making, we can overcome the obstacles that stand in our way and achieve the success we desire.

I think that this is the one chapter that could benefit the most people simply because people rarely decide anything when it comes to their lives.

Many of us will get up in the morning and let the weather decide how we are going to feel. We let the actions of others on the way to work shape how we feel for the rest of the day. Worst of all, many of us take our cues on how to live our lives based on what our friends and family are doing.

If we really stop to think about it, most of our decisions every day are reactions to what's going on around us. Many people, when they do finally decide on anything, are blown completely off course by the slightest wind, which might simply come in the form of a negative comment.

Post on Facebook that you got a job, and people will like, love, and rejoice that you have done the same thing as everyone else. Try posting that you are thinking about setting up a new business or moving countries, and wait for the many reasons it will never work.

People do not do this because they do not like you; it simply comes down to the biological part of the brain that says that if you leave the tribe, you will most likely die. This is not likely going to be the case in modern times, but the instinct is still there.

In many cases people don't want you to succeed because they might simply lose you as a friend if you become rich and end up with a new social circle. It could be as simple as them being jealous that you are brave enough to do something they wish they could.

Knowing why people do things allows you to follow through on your decisions and not take anything they do or say personally.

Making a decision and sticking with it is one of the most important skills you will learn in *Think and Grow Rich*, and this ability will become a huge part of your eventual success.

8: Persistence

If the first plan which you adopt does not work successfully, replace it with a new plan; if this new plan fails to work, replace it in turn with still another, and so on, until you find a plan which does work. Right here is the point at which the majority of men meet with failure, because of their lack of persistence in creating new plans to take the place of those which fail.

—Napoleon Hill

Napoleon now stresses the importance of persistence in achieving success. He argues that persistence is what separates successful people from those who give up in the face of challenges and setbacks.

Hill defines persistence as "the sustained effort necessary to induce faith" and emphasizes that successful people never give up on their goals. He also argues that persistence is a habit that can be developed and strengthened through practice.

Bob also believed that persistence is the key to overcoming obstacles and achieving our goals and that it is a habit that can be developed through consistent practice.

He showed us how successful people never give up on their goals, no matter how difficult or challenging the journey may be. He taught us that persistence requires a clear vision of our goals, a burning desire to achieve them, and a willingness to take consistent action towards them.

By stressing the importance of positive self-talk in developing the habit of persistence, he shows us that our thoughts and beliefs play a crucial role in determining our level of persistence. We must also cultivate a positive mindset to stay focused and motivated in the face of challenges and setbacks.

For anyone looking to achieve their goals and live a fulfilling life, this chapter provides practical strategies for developing the habit of persistence and overcoming the obstacles that stand in the way. By mastering the art of persistence, we can achieve the success we desire and live the life we envision for ourselves.

I love the chapter on persistence, as it is the energy that keeps the other principles moving forward. After having four children, I fully appreciate persistence and its power more now than at any other time in my life.

"Daddy, Daddy, Daddy, Daddy, Daddy", is the theme tune of persistence if ever there was one. In a way, persistence reminds me of imagination in that it is in abundance during our childhood, but somewhere along the way it shrinks or goes into hibernation, often never to return.

I have had to persist many times over the years, and ultimately, I succeeded when I thought I had passed the point of failure.

One more house call at 11:00 p.m. on a Friday night when I was selling insurance, one more late-night viewing when I was showing property, or one more sales call has often been the difference between me and my peers.

In four different industries, in different countries, I became the company's number one in sales, and I put a lot of that down to my own persistence and decision to achieve it.

Bob Proctor would have called me an "unconscious competent". I instinctively knew some of the thirteen principles but didn't know all of them or how to make them work together.

There is a wonderful story in *Think and Grow Rich* about a man who gave up digging when he was three feet from gold. No matter what you do in life, whether it be health, family, or wealth related, never be three feet from gold and always persist. It's always worth that extra push in the end.

9: The Power of the Mastermind

No two minds ever come together without, thereby, creating a third, invisible, intangible force which may be likened to a third mind.

—Napoleon Hill

Now we are introduced to the concept of the mastermind group as a powerful tool for achieving success. Hill defines the *mastermind* as "coordination of knowledge and effort, in a spirit of harmony, between two or more people for the attainment of a definite purpose".

He emphasizes that the mastermind group allows individuals to leverage the knowledge, skills, and resources of others to achieve their goals more effectively and efficiently. He also notes that the mastermind group provides a supportive environment for individuals to bounce ideas off each other, gain new perspectives, and receive feedback.

Bob's view on the Mastermind is that no one achieves success alone and that we all need the support and collaboration of others to reach our full potential.

He emphasized that the mastermind group allows us to tap into the collective intelligence and creativity of others and can help us overcome our limitations and achieve our goals more quickly and easily. He also notes that the mastermind group provides a sense of accountability and motivation, as we are surrounded by like-minded individuals who share our goals and aspirations.

He explains that the key to creating a successful mastermind group is to choose the right people to participate. He notes that the members of the group should share a common purpose and vision and that they should be committed to supporting and challenging each other to achieve their goals.

This chapter provides us with valuable insights into the power of the mastermind group as a tool for achieving success. We are offered practical strategies for creating and leveraging the power of the mastermind group. By working together with others in a spirit of harmony and cooperation, we can achieve greater success than we ever could alone.

When *Think and Grow Rich* was written, the only way people could mastermind was to get on a horse or early car, drive to each other, and sit in a room. Through technology, we can now mastermind with people all over the world in a matter of seconds, but many people still don't do it.

Instead, we sit behind a screen sharing our thoughts through emojis or text messages. We never get to see the real emotion on someone's face or share in thoughts at the same time. My advice is always to go and have that coffee with someone if you can, send a text message, make a phone call or Zoom call and start to mastermind with everyone on every subject.

Over the years, I have worked with people in over one hundred countries, and the strongest relationships and most success I have ever had were with the people I went to see in person. Secondary to this was video conferencing and lastly email.

Marconi sent messages through the air that we could not see, and I firmly believe that the principle of the mastermind works the same when we are communicating with each other in real-time.

When we are on the phone, on Zoom, or in person, we talk about how we feel the conversation went. We use the word feeling to describe our conscious awareness of our own vibrations. Most of our actual communication is nonverbal and we speak to each other via signals we cannot see.

If our mind is like a computer, then joining it up with other minds can turn them into a supercomputer so that all of the knowledge and experience can be pooled, shared, and amplified. The collective power can create ideas and solutions that may never have been possible for someone operating alone. In two companies I previously worked with, we had a "council" of top performers who would regularly get together and share successes and ideas. Some companies do it with area managers, governments do it with special advisors, and you can mastermind with your partner or family member.

What is important to take away from this chapter is that you will get the big results when you reach out and use the mastermind principle as part of your plan for success.

10: The Mystery of Sex Transmutation

Transmutation of sex energy calls for more willpower than the average person cares to use for this purpose.

—Napoleon Hill

Napoleon Hill introduces the concept of *sex transmutation* as a powerful force for achieving success. He defines sex transmutation as "the switching of the mind from thoughts of physical expression to thoughts of some other nature."

He emphasizes that sexual energy is one of the most powerful forms of energy that we possess and that it can be harnessed and redirected towards the achievement of our goals. He notes that many of history's most successful individuals, such as Thomas Edison and Henry Ford, were known for their strong sexual energy and their ability to channel it towards their work.

Bob also taught us that sexual energy is a form of creative energy and that it can be used to fuel our thoughts, ideas, and actions towards the achievement of our goals.

He explained that the key to harnessing the power of sex transmutation is to learn how to control and direct our sexual energy. He explained that this requires discipline, focus, and a clear understanding of our goals and desires.

He also noted that sex transmutation can be used in many different areas of our lives, not just in business or career success. He emphasized that it can be used to enhance our relationships, our health, and our overall well-being.

Sex transmutation is a force for achieving success, and this chapter shows us how to use it to fuel our dreams and aspirations. By learning how to control and direct this powerful force, we can achieve greater success and fulfilment than we ever thought possible.

I think most of us can think of examples of people who have a lot of sexual energy and who are also very successful. This energy can be used as a force for good but unfortunately can be misused too. I enjoy doing work as a film extra as a hobby, and last year I played a nobleman in Ridley Scott's *Napoleon*. If you want an example of someone who used his sexual energy to achieve massive results, the emperor certainly did that!

When he met his wife, Josephine, Napoleon was little more than an unemployed Corsican officer. Just four years later he was ruling France and taking over other countries, driven on by his intense love affair. We know about this thanks to the many love letters he wrote to her from around the world, which have inspired countless books and films on their lives.

What was most interesting for me in the book was that in almost all cases, the men featured did not become successful until they had reached their forties. From a personal perspective, I can relate in that a lot of my energy was misused in my twenties and early thirties on socialising, cars, and dare I say, the pursuit of the fairer sex.

Since getting married I have been able to redirect that energy into my work and family, and I have had my greatest financial and personal successes ever since.

As we end this chapter, think about your own sexual energy and drive and whether you are using it in the right way to get the outcomes you desire.

11: The Subconscious Mind

The subconscious mind is more susceptible to influence by impulses of thought mixed with "feeling" or emotion, than by those originating solely in the reasoning portion of the mind.

—Napoleon Hill

In this chapter, Napoleon Hill delves into the power of the subconscious mind and how it influences our thoughts, beliefs, and actions. He notes that the subconscious mind is responsible for our habits, our emotions, and our behaviours and that it plays a critical role in shaping our reality.

Bob constantly reminded us of the importance of understanding the subconscious mind in achieving success. He explained that our conscious mind is only a small part of our overall awareness and that the subconscious mind is far more powerful and influential than we may realize. He helped us understand that the subconscious mind is like a computer and that it is programmed by our thoughts, beliefs, and experiences. He emphasized that if we want to achieve success, we must learn how to reprogram our subconscious minds with positive thoughts and beliefs.

We need to be mindful that the subconscious mind is always working, even when we're not aware of it. We can use techniques like visualization and affirmations to direct the power of the subconscious mind towards our goals and desires.

The subconscious mind, therefore, influences every aspect of our lives. By learning how to reprogram our subconscious minds with positive thoughts and beliefs, we can achieve greater success and fulfilment than we ever thought possible.

Over 80 percent of the tasks we do every day are automatic and a result of this programming or paradigm. As Robert A. Heinlein, an American science fiction writer, brilliantly put it: "In the absence of clearly defined goals, we become strangely loyal to performing daily trivia until, ultimately, we become enslaved by it".

Many of these are habits we learned from our parents and childhood, and unfortunately, not all are good for us. A lot of what is going into our subconscious mind comes from TV, social media, and unhealthy sources. Think of this information like weeds growing in the garden of your mind that lead to unhappiness, depression, and disease.

In my view, and that of Bob, *disease* is a body which is not at ease! Negative emotions are physically expressed in physical form. Ever notice how people who are depressed are always sick, yet people with a cheerful disposition never seem to be ill? The answer from big pharma is to treat us with drugs or anti-depressants, which kill the weeds but also the soil. By understanding the subconscious and planting good seeds, watering and taking care of them, eventually the weeds will have no room to grow.

With repetition, we can protect our subconscious by being aware of it and standing guard at the door of our mind. We can change the programming, clean the soil, and hard wire in some new beneficial habits that can change our lives for the better. This chapter shows us how to do it.

Start with being grateful for everything you have, write it down, and do something that makes you feel 1 percent better every day.

Little by little, a little becomes a lot!

—Tanzanian proverb

You won't change your subconscious mind in a day or week, but you can start today, and in a year's time, you will be so glad you did.

12: The Brain

You have a brain and mind of your own. Use it and reach your own decisions.

—Napoleon Hill

Napoleon next discusses the role of the brain in achieving success. He notes that the brain is a powerful tool that can be used to achieve any goal, but that it must be trained and developed to be effective. Napoleon knew a lot about the brain, and Bob knew even more, but we still have a long way to go in understanding its capabilities.

Bob explains that the brain is like a muscle and that it must be exercised and trained to achieve its full potential. He emphasizes that the brain is capable of extraordinary feats, but that it must be properly nourished and developed to function at its best.

He notes that the brain is responsible for our thoughts, our beliefs, and our actions and that we can use techniques like visualization and affirmation to direct its power towards our goals and desires. He emphasized that by understanding the science behind how the brain works, we can unlock it and achieve greater success than we ever thought possible.

The brain is constantly changing and evolving, and we can use techniques like meditation and positive thinking to rewire our brains and create new neural pathways that support our goals and desires. By learning how to use the power of our brains, we can achieve any goal and create the life we truly desire.

By the end of this chapter, you will appreciate the power of the brain and how it influences our thoughts, beliefs, and actions. By understanding the science behind how the brain works and learning how to train and develop it through techniques like visualization, affirmations, and meditation, we can achieve greater success and fulfilment.

As Bob Proctor noted, "The brain is the most powerful tool you possess. Use it wisely, and it will take you places beyond your wildest dreams."

As I write this book in 2023, we know a lot more about the brain than we did in 1937, yet there is so much more to learn. We do know that it is the most powerful supercomputer ever built and that no matter how good AI becomes, it will never be able to do something our brain can, and that is originate thought.

The one thing that separates us from all the other animals is that our brain allows us to create a new idea or image that has never been thought of before. AI creates something based on data input, while HI or *human intelligence* can summon new ideas from sources we know little about. It is my belief, as it was Bob's, that our brain is the switching station that connects us to infinite intelligence, God, or whatever term you prefer to use.

Think about the brain originating ideas like this: Many people regard an original painting as the physical object they hang on the wall, when in fact the original painting was created in the artist's mind in the form of a picture. You and I can create whatever pictures we want, pictures that have never been seen before.

As of the time of writing, a computer cannot read your mind, and I hope, for all our sakes, that this sentence ages well. For now, this chapter helps us appreciate that we can create our own reality, and it is our brain that gives us the power to do it.

Over the past ten years, I have used my brain to create images of homes, cars, situations, events, and circumstances that ultimately came true in my life. One of the best examples was imagining the house I wanted us to live in with a tree-lined drive, big gardens, and electric gates. This was a tall order considering we had just stretched to move out of our apartment, but I decided to test the principles and Bob's teaching.

Within twelve months we were living in a six-bedroom Victorian manor house, on seventy acres of land with a beautiful tree-lined lane and those electric gates. The series of events that led us to that would be unbelievable to most, but not to someone who understands and applies the thirteen principles.

While living there I created an image of a beautiful villa overlooking the sea where Emma could walk into the water and swim every day. I knew the warmer climate and salt water would be much better for her health, especially the arthritis, so I got emotionally involved in that image and idea. It is from that property that I am writing this book today.

My only challenge is to keep creating new, bigger, and better images, which I get to do using my fantastic brain. Try it for yourself; imagine where you would like to be in twelve months' time, create some fantastic pictures, and get emotionally involved with them today.

13: The Sixth Sense

Infinite intelligence may, and will communicate voluntarily, without any effort from, or demands by, the individual.

—Napoleon Hill

Hill next explores the concept of the *sixth sense* – the ability to tap into our intuition and inner guidance to make better decisions and achieve greater success.

Napoleon believed that the sixth sense is not something mystical or supernatural, but rather a natural ability that we all possess to varying degrees. It can be developed and honed through techniques such as meditation, introspection, and the practice of mindfulness. According to Hill, the sixth sense operates through our subconscious mind, which is a vast storehouse of knowledge and experience that we can tap into when we learn to silence our conscious thoughts and allow our intuition to guide us.

One of the best ways to develop our sixth sense is to cultivate a deep sense of self-awareness. This means paying attention to our thoughts, emotions, and physical sensations and learning to interpret the signals our body is sending us. By tuning into our inner guidance, we can make better decisions, avoid obstacles, and stay on track towards our goals.

Another important aspect of the sixth sense is the ability to tap into the collective wisdom of others. This is what we learned about earlier in the chapter on the mastermind. By tapping into the collective wisdom of others, we can expand our own knowledge and insight and accelerate our progress towards success.

This chapter reminds us that the sixth sense is a powerful tool for achieving success in any area of life. By developing our intuition, cultivating self-awareness, and tapping into the collective wisdom of others, we can overcome obstacles, make better decisions, and achieve our goals with greater clarity and purpose. As Bob would say, "The sixth sense is like a compass that guides us towards our true purpose in life. Trust it, cultivate it, and watch as your life unfolds in magical and unexpected ways."

Many of us may understand our sixth sense as our gut instinct. I like to call it my *God instinct* because I have grown to master and trust it, but mainly because it is almost always right. "Let go and let God," is a famous verse many of us will have heard. For me it is an instruction to listen to your sixth sense and act on it, *act* being the important word. Once you start to do that and begin to trust, your sixth sense can be a wonderful torch guiding you to success.

I believe our sixth sense is a culmination of our six "higher faculties" that we as humans possess that separate us from the animal kingdom.

You already know about our five senses, our ability to see, smell, hear, taste, and touch, but our cat Cookie has those too. The following senses are the ones we need to be aware of if we are going to tap into our sixth sense:

1. Imagination
2. Will
3. Perception
4. Intuition
5. Reason
6. Memory

Imagine where you want to be in a year's time. No one else can do that except you.

Use your **will** to persist when everyone else would give up.

Perceive how you think a situation will play out before it happens.

Does your **intuition** tell you when the phone is about to ring?

Do you ever **reason** with anyone to help them see a new point of view?

Your **memory** helps you see images that no one on earth can ever see!

Spend some time every day, get to know these faculties, and use these superpowers that most people take for granted. Once you do, you will start to enjoy using them. I certainly do!

Chapter 7
Outwitting the Six Ghosts of Fear

(Chapter 15 in *Think and Grow Rich*)

This chapter focuses on how to outwit the six ghosts of fear, another thing few of us are consciously aware of.

Fear is a common emotion that can hold us back from succeeding and realizing our potential. However, Napoleon Hill argues that fear can be overcome through a combination of awareness and action.

The six ghosts of fear that Hill identifies are as follows:

- Fear of poverty

- Fear of criticism

- Fear of ill health

- Fear of loss of love

- Fear of old age

- Fear of death

Hill emphasizes that these fears are not imaginary but rather exist within our minds and can hold us back from achieving our goals. He encourages readers to confront their fears head-on and take action to eliminate them completely.

To overcome the fear of poverty, Hill suggests taking steps to become financially independent, such as investing in oneself and taking risks in business ventures.

To overcome the fear of criticism, Hill recommends developing self-confidence and not letting the opinions of others hold us back.

To overcome the fear of ill health, Hill advocates maintaining a healthy lifestyle and seeking medical treatment when needed.

To overcome the fear of loss of love, Hill suggests maintaining positive relationships with loved ones while also focusing on personal growth and development.

To overcome the fear of old age, Hill encourages readers to focus on personal growth and continue learning throughout their lives.

Finally, to overcome the fear of death, Hill suggests adopting a positive attitude towards life and focusing on the present moment rather than worrying about the future.

Hill also emphasizes the importance of faith and belief in oneself when confronting these fears. He believes that by taking action and having faith in oneself, anyone can overcome their fears and achieve their goals.

Bob always explained that the antidote to fear is faith. In an absence of faith, the void is filled with fear, and both cannot exist in the same place. It could also be said that fear comes from a lack of understanding or information about something. If you have the education and knowledge, that can be enough to eliminate the fear.

On my own journey I have discovered that these specific "ghosts" Napoleon mentions are part genetic and part environmental. If we understand the biological reasons, then we can overcome them much faster.

Throughout human history we have been a species who lived in social groups where leaving that group would almost certainly mean death by starvation or possibly a sabre-toothed tiger!

This is why criticism hurts so badly, whether it be online or in person: criticism is designed to keep us together.

Even though we are now living in modern society, this chimp part of our brain remains, and it as strong as ever. We simply need to learn to differentiate between what the human brain and the chimp brain are telling us.

If you want to keep the chimp part of your brain happy and leave room for the human side to make good decisions, make sure the chimp side doesn't get lonely, angry, hungry, or tired. There is a wonderful book called *The Chimp Paradox* by Steve Peters if you want to know more about this fascinating subject.

Fortunately for the human species, a percentage of all humans have a certain amount of what we would now call *ADHD genes*, and these brains are wired not to listen, to explore and take risks.

Thanks to these people, some of our ancestors left the tribe, found new mates, discovered new lands, and populated the earth, ensuring our species' survival.

As an Irishman, I think about the millions of people who left the Emerald Isle and set sail to unknown lands on one-way tickets to survive or even make their fortune. They had desire, imagination, persistence, and faith and overcame the six ghosts of fear.

We all can if we understand what these fears are. It is much easier to be aware of them and defeat them with faith, persistence, auto-suggestion, and reason.

I had my own struggles with all these ghosts, and still do every now and again. The difference now is that I have strategies to recognise and overcome them should they reappear.

Success is not a straight line; you may take three steps forward and two back, and that's fine as long as you are constantly moving forward.

You will find that as you become aware, you can master these ghosts and enjoy your life to the fullest. These are universal fears, and *Think and Grow Rich* provides universal solutions to overcome them.

Chapter 8

Unlocking Potential: Breaking Free From the "Fifty-Seven Famous Alibis" by Old Man If

Among the many valuable lessons from Hill's seminal work, the "Fifty-Seven Famous Alibis" by Old Man If holds a mirror to our own self-imposed limitations. This section unravels the common excuses that shackle us, preventing us from realizing our dreams.

Imagine them as stories we tell ourselves to make us feel better about the situation we don't want to be in.

As I write this in modern times, there are many more alibis I could add relating to things such as technology, gender, age, and race, but for now let's take the list from the book. They are just as relevant today as they were in 1937.

Have a look to see if you have ever said them or heard them from someone else:

1. "If I didn't have a wife and family ..."

2. "If I had enough 'pull"... '

3. "If I had money ..."

4. "If I had a good education ..."

5. "If I could get a job ..."

6. "If I had good health ..."

7. "If I only had time ..."

8. "If times were better . . ."

9. "If other people understood me . . ."

10. "If conditions around me were only different . . ."

11. "If I could live my life over again . . ."

12. "If I did not fear what 'they' would say . . ."

13. "If I had been given a chance . . ."

14. "If I now had a chance . . ."

15. "If other people didn't 'have it in for me'' . . ."

16. "If nothing happens to stop me . . ."

17. "If I were only younger . . ."

18. "If I could only do what I want . . ."

19. "If I had been born rich . . ."

20. "If I could meet 'the right people'' . . ."

21. "If I had the talent that some people have . . ."

22. "If I dared assert myself . . ."

23. "If I only had embraced past opportunities . . ."

24. "If people didn't get on my nerves . . ."

25. "If I didn't have to keep house and look after the children . . ."

26. "If I could save some money . . ."

27. "If the boss only appreciated me . . ."

28. "If I only had somebody to help me . . ."

29. "If my family understood me . . ."

30. "If I lived in a big city . . ."

31. "If I could just get started . . ."

32. "If I were only free . . ."

33. "If I had the personality of some people . . ."

34. "If I were not so fat . . ."

35. "If my talents were known . . ."

36. "If I could just get a 'break' . . . '

37. "If I could only get out of debt . . ."

38. "If I hadn't failed . . ."

39. "If I only knew how . . ."

40. "If everybody didn't oppose me . . ."

41. "If I didn't have so many worries . . ."

42. "If I could marry the right person . . ."

43. "If people weren't so dumb . . ."

44. "If my family weren't so extravagant . . ."

45. "If I were sure of myself . . ."

46. "If luck were not against me . . ."

47. "If I had not been born under the wrong star . . ."

48. "If it were not true that 'what is to be, will be'... '

49. "If I did not have to work so hard ..."

50. "If I hadn't lost my money ..."

51. "If I lived in a different neighbourhood ..."

52. "If I didn't have a 'past'... '

53. "If I only had a business of my own ..."

54. "If other people would only listen to me ..."

55. "If, and this is the greatest of them all, I had the courage to see myself as I really am, I would find out what is wrong with me, and correct it, then I might have a chance to profit by my mistakes and learn something from the experience of others, for I know that there is something WRONG with me, or I would now be where I WOULD HAVE BEEN IF I had spent more time analysing my weaknesses, and less time building alibis to cover them."

56. "If I had the courage to undertake the self-analysis it would be so easy for me to stop and find out what is wrong with me, but that is exactly what I will not do, well, because ..."

57. "If I knew exactly why I hold on to my alibis so stoutly I could probably throw them off. I never had the courage to consider the procedure. I will not investigate the possibility of self-analysis and really find out what is wrong with me, because ..."

I will expand on two, and then try to repeat the process yourself with the remaining alibis. You will see that, with a little analysis, you can quickly make them disappear.

1.   "If I didn't have a wife and family ..." – Many blame family

responsibilities for their lack of success. Yet successful people have proved that one can build wealth while nurturing a family. It's not about choosing between the two; it's about striking the right balance.

I started my Think and Grow Rich journey with a chronically ill wife, a young son, and another baby on the way. My wife was unable to work, and we had no money to buy food, let alone pay rent.

Not only did I succeed, but we also had two more children, and within six years I had built multiple businesses and was travelling the world speaking to audiences of up to four thousand people.

The best piece of advice I can give anyone is that there will never be a right time to do anything. You must start where you are and move towards your goal right now.

Everything you need will be supplied to you to ensure you are successful. Just trust the process. Napoleon, Bob, I, and countless others over the years have proven that it works every time.

In the words of Martin Luther King Jr: "You don't need to see the whole staircase, just take the first step".

1. "If I had enough 'pull' . . ." – Pull or influence is something one can build over time through sincere efforts and building relationships. It shouldn't be seen as a deterrent, but as a goal to strive for.

Through similar analysis, we can dissect each of the "Fifty-Seven Famous Alibis". As Bob Proctor always says, our greatest power is the ability to change. By recognizing and overcoming these alibis, we can tap into our infinite potential.

Hill presents us with a list of alibis, not to invite excuses, but to show us the path beyond them. When we free ourselves from these self-imposed limitations, we clear the path for success, wealth, and abundance to find us.

Unshackle your potential and break free from the chains of these alibis. They are myths, mirages, stories you are telling yourself that have no basis in reality. That is because *reality* is what you decide it to be. Every day is a new fresh page of your life; yesterday doesn't exist except in your memory. The good news is you are holding the pen for today's page, and you can decide what is written on it.

Chapter 9

Transcending the Ordinary – Embracing the Power of Think and Grow Rich

As we draw this enriching journey to a close, it is apt to bring the curtains down by reflecting upon the profound wisdom imparted by Napoleon Hill's immortal work. This masterpiece has served as our guiding light, a compass that pointed us towards the true north of personal and financial success. It has ushered us on a transformative odyssey, revealing the infinite possibilities that lie dormant within the depths of our consciousness.

Hill's magnum opus hinges on a "definite chief aim." He calls upon us to gaze inward, to find that one audacious aspiration that sets our hearts ablaze. It could be as grand as a business empire, or as simple as a serene home in the countryside. Regardless of its nature, Hill urges us to etch this dream onto our minds, to treat it as our guiding star in life's grand voyage.

Hill uncovered for us the profound powers of faith and belief, the invisible hands that shape our destinies. He imparted an empowering truth that the subconscious mind, once programmed with our desires and unflinching belief, can propel us towards our dreams. When nurtured with relentless positivity and unwavering confidence, our subconscious mind becomes an invincible ally that forges our path towards triumph.

Yet on this voyage to success, Hill reminds us of the significance of persistence. There are no express lanes or shortcuts on this journey, only a winding path peppered with challenges and setbacks. We must just remember that these obstacles are not our enemies. They are opportunities, wrapped in a rough exterior, that test our resolve and refine us. They mould us into relentless warriors, ready to conquer our dreams.

Hill then introduced us to the concept of a mastermind group, a collective of fervent minds, united by common objectives, pooling their knowledge, experiences, and ideas. The energy that such a group creates can catalyse our individual dreams, accelerating us towards our goals at unprecedented speed.

The discussion on the power of the subconscious mind is where Hill beautifully intertwines the scientific with the spiritual. Positive affirmations and visualization techniques, he suggests, can reprogram our subconscious mind, making it a magnet that attracts success and wealth.

Finally, Hill unveiled for us the pinnacle of his philosophy – the sixth sense. It is the ultimate stage of mental evolution, where our conscious and subconscious minds unite. This fusion produces a mysterious yet powerful force – intuition. This sixth sense can guide us with hunches and gut feelings, playing an essential role on our journey towards success.

And so, as we conclude our journey through Hill's timeless classic, let us remember that we are not just passive readers. We are pioneers, ready to apply these enlightening principles to our lives. We are the creators of our destiny, equipped with the power of thought, the tool that can sculpt a life of limitless abundance and prosperity.

As Bob used to say, *Think and Grow Rich* should not merely be read; it should be lived. Let the seeds of its wisdom be planted deep within your mind. Nurture them with unwavering belief and committed action. Then behold the miracle as they sprout into a life of boundless abundance and unparalleled success.

Napoleon Hill's journey of discovery began around 1910 and lasted until 1970, Bob's from 1961 until 2022, and mine started in 2013. As I write this book, aged just forty-five, my dream is to have a positive effect as those two great men did and share this great work with as many people around the globe as possible. Through social media, video, and other resources not available to Napoleon Hill, I can bring this information to a new and greater audience.

Make sure to share this book with as many people as you can and to read or listen to Napoleon's full work as soon as possible. Read it often and be amazed at the new wisdom you receive each time as you reach a new floor on the skyscraper of consciousness.

Let this be not the end, but the beginning of your journey towards your dreams. May this book and the power of *Think and Grow Rich* illuminate your path as you step forward to manifest your life's grandest desires.

Chapter 10
How to Get a Life

One day I when I was doing some private coaching, I asked someone what they really wanted, and they replied that they wanted to "get a life".

It's a phrase we all know, and so I thought it would be a great title to help me share my knowledge on the very subjects which might help others get a life.

It is not called "get *the* life" because not everyone wants money and fame or what someone else would deem as success. You must identify what will make you happy and go after the life you want.

Bob often quoted Bill Gove as saying, "If I want to be free I gotta be me. Not the me I think you think I should be, not the me that I think my wife wants to me or the me that I think my kids want me to be. I gotta be me, so I better know who me is".

How do you find out who "me" is?

Start by writing down what your ideal day, week, month, and year looks like in vivid detail, and get emotionally involved in those ideas.

What time would you get up? What would you eat? How often would you exercise? Would you learn a language, instrument, or how to paint? Who would you spend more or less time with? Where would you like to visit?

If there are material things you would like to have, then go to the dealership and sit in the car you want to own, smell it, and feel it. Do a viewing on your ideal home for the same reasons.

Plan out your dream trip and cost it out. If any of this makes you feel uncomfortable, that's good. It must be a real goal, and you are on the right path.

Feeling is simply the conscious awareness of the vibration you are in. As the Beach Boys would say, "Get in a good vibration".

Next write out a goal card, putting it all into the present tense: "I am so happy and grateful now that . . ."

I started this process in 2013 and still do it every day. Every time I reach a goal, I create a bigger one. As I write this book, my goal is to train mentors in this subject and have at least one in every country on earth.

If you would like to join me on this journey, please check out the following resources and contacts:

Website – https://getalife.info

Facebook https://facebook.com/bmcglife

Instagram – https://instagram.com/getalife.info

TikTok – https://tiktok.com/@getalife.info

Twitter https://twitter.com/bmcglife

Reading List

Over the past ten years Bob introduced me to many books that have helped me lead a better, healthier, and happier life. I have listed the most impactful of these below in chronological order.

As an Audible user, I listened to them as they were recommended but realise now that it would make more sense to do it in the order they were written. This is because you will hear echoes from the past in each one as the layers of information are built upon and science advances through the decades:

As a Man Thinketh – James Allen 1902

The Science of Getting Rich – Wallace Wattles 1910

The Master Key System – Charles F Haanel – 1916

Think and Grow Rich – Napoleon Hill – 1937

The Strangest Secret – Earl Nightingale – 1957

Psycho-Cybernetics – Maxwell Maltz 1960

The Power of Your Subconscious Mind – Joseph Murphy – 1963

Lead the Field – Earl Nightingale – 1968

You Were Born Rich – Bob Proctor – 1984

The Four Agreements – Don Miguel Ruiz -1997

Unleash the Power Within – Tony Robbins – 1999

The Secret – Rhonda Byrne – 2006

I will leave you with a poem that Napoleon mentions in the book and one I think sums up a lot of *Think and Grow Rich*:

The Man Who Thinks He Can

If you think you are beaten, you are,

If you think you dare not, you don't,

If you like to win, but you think you can't,

It is almost certain you won't.

If you think you'll lose, you're lost,

For out of the world we find,

Success begins with a fellow's will,

It's all in the state of mind.

If you think you are outclassed, you are,

You've got to think high to rise,

You've got to be sure of yourself before,

You can ever win a prize.

Life's battles don't always go,

To the stronger or faster man,

But soon or late the man who wins,

Is the man who thinks he can.

– Walter D Wintle

Don't miss out!

Visit the website below and you can sign up to receive emails whenever BMcGinty publishes a new book. There's no charge and no obligation.

https://books2read.com/r/B-A-XQCZ-UFUKC

BOOKS 2 READ

Connecting independent readers to independent writers.

About the Author

Happy husband and father of four. Mentor, Consultant, Author, and world explorer.

Read more at https://getalife.info.